Sri Tallapaka Annamacharya

Bio Horoscope

(Astrology Prediction Analysis)

By

Suripeddi Koundinya

[M.A Astrology]

శ్రీ తాళ్ళపాక అన్నమాచార్య

Sri Tallapaka Annamacharya was the 15th Century Saint Telugu Composer, who composed 36,000 Keertana Songs (of which only 12,000 are available today) which influenced the Carnatic Music. He extolled as *"Andhra Padakavita Pitamaha"*, hailed from Kadapa dist., of Andhra Pradesh (A.P).

His compositions were forgotten over three centuries until found engraved on copper plates in 1849, which was hidden for centuries inside the **Sri Venkateswara Swami temple** at Tirumala, just opposite the Hundi, concealed in a very small room.

He also wrote 12 Satakas but only one remains. His other lost works such as *"Dwipada Ramayana, Venkatachala Mahatmyam, Sankirtana Lakshanam, etc."* were written in other languages.

Annamacharya was considered as a great devotee (bhakta) of **Bhagwaan Govinda Venkateshwara** (idol at Tirumala [TTD] place of A.P, India) and also believed to have been the reincarnation of the precious Sword of Lord Vishnu (Nandakam).

For years, there has been a debate about the birth date of Sri Annamayya whether he was born on 09th / 14th / 22nd of May 1408.

After going through his biography, I fixed the date 09th of May, born at afternoon around 12 p.m. Some may argue that he was born in Vishakha star (nakshatram), but to be noted that it was written that his birth was in the masa (month) of Vaishakha (*The name* of *the* month is derived from *the* position of *the* moon near *the* star *Vishakha* on full moon day) which was under the influence of Vishakha nakshatram.

He was born on Vaishakha Shuddha Pournami in the year Sarwadhari in Tallapaka, Near Rajampet Mandal, a village in present-day Kadapa district of Andhra Pradesh, India to the Brahmin couples *Narayana Suri and Lakkamamba.*

శ్రీ తాళ్ళపాక అన్నమాచార్య

Venus Saturn		Sun Mer Jup Rah	Moon
			Mars Ascendant
	\ Rasi \		
	Ketu		

Mercury Ascendant		Moon	
Saturn			Ketu
Sun Rahu	\ Navamsa \		Jupiter
	Venus		Mars

So, Annamayya was born in Cancer Lagna and Moon in Purnarvasu -2 (Gemini sign).

His poetic ability is marked by position of 5th lord Mars in Ascendant (Lagna). He was not only a poet but also a Singer and Musician which is marked by position of 2nd lord Sun with Rahu in Krittika -2 along with Jupiter & Mercury in Taurus (house of Venus).

He always used to hold Tampura (Tambura) to play his tunes and sing songs in the name of Lord Venkateshwara- (Tambura is a long-necked plucked string instrument, originating from India, found in various forms in Indian music).

శ్రీ తాళ్ళపాక అన్నమాచార్య

Remember the symbol of Krittika is an axe, razor or sharp instruments.

The *third and eleventh houses* represent right and left hands of an individual. The third lord Mercury in eleventh house in the star of Krittika shows his expertise in handling and playing musical instruments.

At the early age of 5, He was gifted with intuitive perception (Jupiter dasha – Venus antardasha) as his tutors realized that there is nothing much to teach him. He frequently used to visit the temple of *Lord Chennakesava* and address him "my little kesava".

Annamayya was not used to hard work and was soon getting tired. This is because of debilitated Mars in horoscope. Mars represent energy and vitality.

At a blossom age of 8, he travelled to Tirupati on bare foot along with pilgrimages that were passing through his village. *This occurred at the end of Jupiter Period and Rahu sub-period.*

శ్రీ తాళ్ళపాక అన్నమాచార్య

The main period of Saturn commences to begin which lasts for 19 years.

Upon reaching Tirumala, he visited following Holy Places:

a) Gangamma Goddess

b) Lord Narasimha (4th Incarnation of Lord Vishnu)

c) Idol of Lord Hanuman (Anjaneya) at Taleru Gundu (a magic rock at the foot of Tirumala)

d) Alamelu Manga (damsel standing on a flower) darshan in a Dream

e) Swami Pushkarini (Holy Pond)

f) Lord Adi-Varaha (3rd Incarnation of Lord vishnu)

g) Kumaradhara (where Kumaraswami, son of Lord Siva did penance after killing a demon called Tarakasura)

h) Amarathirtha (where all the Gods bathe everyday)

i) Akasaganga (where Anjana – mother of Lord Hanuman, did Penance for 12 years before giving birth to Anjaneya).

శ్రీ తాళ్ళపాక అన్నమాచార్య

j) Papavinasanam and finally

k) Lord Venkateshwara

I have seen in many charts of those born with combination of *Sun & Rahu* visits pilgrimage places frequently and probably their death occurs there.

He had the darshan of Lord Karthikeya (Kumara swami) also known as Lord Muruga who resides on / deity of Krittika (Pleiades) constellation. – [Jupiter dasha (in Mrigashira - 1) and Rahu antardasha (in Krittika -2)].

Annamayya was anointed for Vaishnavism by Ghana Vishnu (Vaishnava Sage) at Tirumala at age 12. – Saturn Period began.

Saturn in 9th house – Religious madness, along with exalted Venus tells firm faith, devotion and beliefs towards God.

4th lord Venus with Saturn also foretells staying away from homeland.

After a while, his parents visited Tirumala and took Annamacharya along with them to

శ్రీ తాళ్ళపాక అన్నమాచార్య

Tallapaka. He reluctant to go first but God appeared in his dream and told to listen to his parents and stick to attain spirituality.

When Annamayya attained the age of 16 in the year 1424, his parents got him married to two young girls by name Timmakka and Akkalamma. See the position of 7th lord Saturn in 9th H – dual marriage or extra-marital relationship. This happened in Saturn period and Venus sub-period.

At the month of Vaishakha on the event of his birthday in the year 1424, when Annamacharya was alone in the Tirumala temple after worshipping Lord Venkateshwara, and taking rest in the portico adjacent to the temple of Varaha in the night. As he could not sleep and singing a poem in the name of Lord, suddenly Venkateshwara swami appeared before him, blessed him and cited to compose a "Sankirtana" every day for him.

Accordingly, Annamayya composed a song every day as he wandered from place to place.

శ్రీ తాళ్ళపాక అన్నమాచార్య

People who listened to his songs were thrilled with beautiful use of the Telugu idioms and the divine philosophy contained in those songs.

Ascendant lord Moon in 12th house Gemini (Dwiswabava Rashi) and cancer lagna itself is a movable sign – Annamayya used to wander throughout his life, and singing songs in the name of Lord Venkatehwara.

Annamacharya underwent training under *Sage Sathagopa Yati for 12 years,* who resides at the bank of river Bhavanasini at Ahobilam {Allagadda mandal of Kurnool district in the Indian state of Andhra Pradesh.} The sage has received blessings from Lord Narasimha to be an Ascetic.

Annamayya became an enlightened man and aimed to spread the philosophy of Vaishnavism through his sweet songs.

Salva Narasinga Raya, the ruler of Tangutur (a small village in Rajampet taluk) became disciple of Annamacharya. He became king of

Penugonda and requested his Guru to stay there in his kingdom, for which Annamayya accepted to carry on his divine duty of spreading Visishtadwaita philosophy with the royal assistance.

One fine morning, King Narasinga Raya summoned Annamayya to his court and there were his ministers, princes, generals and members of the royal family. The king requested his Guru to compose a song on him. Annamayya got infuriated and stood from his place and left from there. King felt insulted among his subordinates and ordered to imprison Annamayya.

Annamayya was not perturbed by the ill-treatment and appealed to the Lord Venkatapathi of his mercy in a pathetic song. The chains broke and fell down twice in presence of servants as well as King. The king realized his mistake and fell at his feet and begged to forgive him. Annamayya advised King to not to hurt a pious man and devotee of

God. And finally Annamacharya left for Tirumala.

See the position of Lagna lord Moon in 12th H (House of Imprisonment) in the deadly star of Punarvasu and the 12th lord Mercury with Rahu along with Sun, and also debilitated 10th lord Mars – this confers that the person get punishment by King's Wrath.

On his way, he wrote a rimming couplet called "Sringara Manjari".

Annamayya blessed a musician named "Purandara Das" of Karnataka and told that his songs are going to be primary lessons in Carnatic music.

Annammaya's first wife Timmakka was also a Poetess and their sons Peda Tirumalaiah, China Tirumalaiah & Narsinganna also were known as Tallapaka Poets.

His son Chinna Tirumalacharya wrote Annamacharya's biography. The family was evidently well-to-do for there are records of their having donated villages to the Tirumala and other temples for the daily conduct of several rituals. Annamacharya is credited with introducing the ceremonial bathing of Venkateswara every Friday, a practice that continues till date. The descendants of the family are honoured at the temple even today. During his lifetime, Annamacharya was well known. Chinna Tirumalacharya states that Purandara Dasa met Annmacharya and the similarities in the songs *'Sharanu Saranu Surendra Vandita and Saranu Saranu Surendra Sevita'*, respectively by the two composers; both in Malavi Raga are offered as internal evidence. Annamacharya's sons Narasinganna, Chinna Tiruvengalanatha and Pedda Tirumalacharya have been praised as poets and scholars by Tenali Ramakrishna, the scholar of Krishnadeva Raya's court. The icons of Annmacharya and Pedda Tirumalacharya were carved on either side of the first gopuram of the Kalyana Venkateswara shrine in Srinivasa Manga Puram near Tirupati. This was done at the instance of Chinna Tirumalacharya who renovated the temple. An idol of Annamacharya also exists at this temple. This shrine also houses the idols worshipped by Annamacharya's family. The songs of Annamacharya were originally on palm leaf manuscripts. Some of his palm leaf manuscripts are at the Tanjavur Saraswati Mahal Library. His son Pedda Tirumalacharya got them inscribed on copper plates between 1525 and 1545 and these were stored in a chamber called the Sankirtana Bhandaramu in the Tirumala premises.

Later songs and works of other members of the Tallapaka family were also transferred to copper plates and added to this repository. This structure has the statues of Annamacharya and his son Pedda Tirumalacharya on either side.

Annamacharaya Kriti embosed into Copper Plate (Talla patralu)

In 1816, AD Campbell, a Government officer first recorded the existence of these plates and sent a deputation to inspect them. On coming to know that they contained "nothing but voluminous hymns in praise of the Deity", they were left as they were.

A rhyming couplet of poems called "Dwipada" written by Tallapaka Chinnanna, grandson of Annamacharya, enabled us to learn about the Saint Annamacharya, his life and works. Annamacharya was born on

శ్రీ తాళ్ళపాక అన్నమాచార్య

Vaisakhapoornima in the year Sarwadhari (May 9, 1408) in Tallapaka, a remote village in Andhra Pradesh, and lived immaculately for 95 years until Phalguna Bahula Dwadasi (12th day after full moon) in the year Dhundhubhi (February 23, 1503). Annamacharya is believed to be the incarnation of Lord Venkateswara's Nandaka or Sword. Tirumala Tirupati Devasthanams (TTD) have consecrated Annamacharya in two places, one in the Annamacharya Mandiram located in the Annamacharya Project Office premises at Tiruapati and the other one in Annamacharya temple at Tallapka the birth place of Annamcharya. The evidences supporting the fact that Annamacharya is the incarnation of the Lord are found in Chinnanna's Dwipada.

It is believed that in the 10th century a big famine broke out in Varanasi and scores of scholars migrated to southern part of India for earning their livelihoods. Some of them concentrated in a town called "Nandavaram"

శ్రీ తాళ్ళపాక అన్నమాచార్య

in Andhra Pradesh which was ruled by the then king Nanda. These immigrants were called "Nandavarikas" and Annamacharyas forefathers were the so called Nandavarikas and hence Annamacharya.

Tirumala Tirupati Devasthanams, also known as TTD, has been endeavouring to preserve the rich heritage of his compositions. In the year 1950, The State Government of Andhra Pradesh created a committee and appointed Dr M Balamuralikrishna as its head. He set music to over 800 compositions of Sri Annamayya and are still popular among the devotees. He has been the Asthana Gayaka of the Tirumala temple at Tirupati since two decades. He is regarded as a legend in rendering devotional music in classical style, especially the Annamacharya sankirtanas. He is also an acclaimed poet, singer, and a musicologist.

Dr. Shobha Raju is the first recipient of Tirumala Tirupati Devasthanams scholarship in 1976 to study and set a trend for the propagation of Annamacharya's compositions, and was also chosen as the first exclusive artiste for the propagation of Annamacharya's compositions in 1978. Her first audio album, "Venkateswara Geeta Malika" is globally popular among Telugu community. She is the founder of Annamacharya Bhavana Vahini (ABV) in 1983, which is located in Hyderabad, India. She has been awarded Padma Sri by Government of India, in 2010 in recognition of her efforts to promote Annamayya Compositions.

In 1922, twenty five hundred copper plates, comprising of about 14,000 *sankIrtana*s and a few other works, were found in a rock built cell, later named as *Sankirtana Bhandagaram*, opposite to the *Hundi* (donation box).

Ever since the discovery of this lost treasure, Tirumala Tirupati Devastanams (TTD) and other organizations in India are working hard to promote the music and literature of Annamacharya.

<h1 style="text-align:center">శ్రీ తాళ్ళపాక అన్నమాచార్య</h1>

1. **Vinnapalu Vinavaley Vintha Vinthalu**
   Pannagapu Doma Thera Pai Ketha
   Veylayya

Thella Varay Jhamekkay Devathalu Munulu
Allanalla Nanthanintha Adigo Varey
Challani Thammi Rekula Sarasyapu
Gannulu
Mella Mellaney Vichi Melu Kona
Veylayya | Vinnapalu |

Garuda Kinnara Yaksha Kaminulu Gamulai
Virahapu Geethamula Vintha Thalala
Pari Pari Vidhamula Paderu Ninnadivo
Siri Mogamu Derachi Chithagincha
Veylayya | Vinnapalu |

Ponkapu Seshadulu Tumburu Naradadulu
Pankaja Bhavadulu Nee Padalu Cheri
Ankela Nunnaru Lechi Alamelu Manganu
Venkatesuda Reppalu Vichi Choochi
Leyvayya | Vinnapalu |

<u>శ్రీ తాళ్ళపాక అన్నమాచార్య</u>

Annamacharya composed and sang Sankirtanas right from the first service of the day to the last service at night to Lord Venkateswara in Tirumala Temple. Even today, this tradition is being continued in Tirumala Temple. The opening service to the Lord Venkateswara starts with a Melukolupu Sankirtana (Wake up composition) of Annamacharya followed by Suprabhatham and the closing service at night with a Jolapata (lullabye) of Annamacharya during Ekantha Seva

Vinnapaalu Vina Valey Vintha Vinthalu is one of the many Melukolupu Sakirtanas rendered by Annamacharya to Lord Venkateswara. In this composition, Annamcharya sang melodiouly to wake up the Lord Venkateswara to perform the duty of attending to His devotees' requests.

Annamacharya asks the Lord to slowly open His lotus eye lids and look at the sages wo are waiting for Him, Yaksha and Kinnera women *singing in a state of bliss, and Adisesha, Brahma, Narada, Tumbura and others who are rowed at His feet. Annamacharya asks Venkateswara to open His eyes, look at Alamelu Manga and listen to the appeals of all His devotees.*

2. **Anni Manthramulu Yindey Avahinchenu**
   Vennatho Naku Galigey Venkatesu Manthramu

Naradudu Japiyinchey Narayana Manthramu
Cherey Prahladudu Narasimha Manthramu
Kori Vibhishanudu Chekoney Rama Manthramu
Veray Naku Galigey Venkatesu Manthramu | Anni |

Rangagu Vasudeva Manthramu Dhruvudu Japiyinchey
Angavinchey Krishna Manthramu Arjunudu
Mungita Vishnu Manthramu Mogi Sukudu Pathiyinchey

శ్రీ తాళ్ళపాక అన్నమాచార్య

**Vingadamai Naku Nabbay Venkatesu
Manthramu | Anni |**

**Inni Manthramula Kella Indira Nadhudey
Guri
Pannina Didiyey Para Brahma Manthramu
Nannu Gava Galigeybo Naku Guru
Deeyaganu
Vennela Vantidi Sri Venkatesu
Manthramu | Anni |**

This is a composition of Tallapaka Annamcharya. In this composition Annamcaharya says that All Mantras are in Venkatesu Mantra which he acquired as a child.

Naarada chanted Narayana Mantra, Prahlada-Narasimha Mantra, Vibheeshana-Rama Mantra, Dhruva-Vasudeva Mantra, Arjuna-Krishna Mantra, and Sage Suka-Vishnu Mantra.

Lord Vishnu is the focus for all the Mantras and the Vishnu Mantra is the Para Brahma Mantra.

Since Lord Venkateswara is Vishnu, Annamacharya deduces that all Mantras are in Venkatesu Mantra which is as cool as the Moonlight. (In another composition Annamacharya describes the qualities of Moonlight, which explains why Annamacharya established similarity between Venkatesu Mantra and Moonlight)

3. **Hari Yavathara**
   Meethadu   Annamayya

   Araya Ma
   Gurdeethadu   Annamayya

Vaikuntha Nadhuni Vadda   Vadi Padu Chunna Vadu
Akaramai Thallapaka   Annamayya
Akasapu Vishnu Pada Mandu   Nithyamai Yunna Vadu
Akadeekada   Thallapaka
Annamayya |
Hariyava |

Eevala Samsara Leela   Indirisu Tho Nunna Vadu
Avatinchi Thallapaka   Annamayya
Bhavimpa Sri Venkatesu   Padamulanday Yunnavadu

Hava Bhavamai Thallapaka Annamayya | Hariyava |

This is a composition of Tallapaka Chinnanna, the grandson of Annamacharya. Annamacharya's son Pedda Tirumalacharya and grandson Chinnanna were also great composers and musicians.

In this composition, Chinnanna honors his grand father Annamacharya by calling him the incarnation of Hari or Vishnu.

Brief escence of this composition is:

Annamacharya is the incarnation of Hari and he is our Guru. He is singing the glory of Lord Vishnu at His abode, Annamacharya resides at the Lotus feet of Lord Sri Venkateswara or Vishnu.

Om Namo Venkatesaya

www.ingramcontent.com/pod-product-compliance
Lightning Source LLC
Chambersburg PA
CBHW020857160726
47993CB00004B/1706